GREAT MARQUES POSTER BOOK

PORSCHE

CHRIS HARVEY

WOODBURY PRESS

Introduction

Porsche have advanced, in under 40 years, from producing a simple sports car, using whatever bits and pieces of old Volkswagens were to hand, to being the most important producer of sporting vehicles and components in the world today. The reason for its success is that Porsche has always had as its hall mark that brand of perfectionism that results in very good, reliable, vehicles that perform outstandingly, despite accusations that most of them have had their engines in the wrong place!

The classic rear-engined Porsche has its roots in the Volkswagen Beetle designed before the Second World War by Professor Ferdinand Porsche. His reason for positioning the engine behind the rear wheels was partly to give the car better traction over the exceedingly rough and steep roads it was expected to encounter (especially in its native Austria) and partly to leave as much room as possible for passengers and luggage. Following this line of thought, the main Porsche production cars, the Type 356 of 1948 to 1965 and the Type 911 that was first produced in 1964 and continues at the top of the range today, have succeeded as a result of dedicated research and development which overcame handling quirks caused by having the front wheels lightly loaded.

Oddly enough, the very first Porsche, a sports racing model built in 1948, had its Volkswagen power train reversed to give a mid-engined installation. This was deemed ideal for competition by Professor Porsche, as it gave more even weight distribution, and the fact that it occupied valuable passenger space didn't of course matter. But the second Porsche – a road-going model – had the engine back behind the rear wheels. After that, the ageing professor had little to do with the cars that bore his name. He was unwell, partly as a result of being imprisoned in France after the war and getting back to Austria only after his son, also called Ferdinand, had earned enough from helping design an Italian national racing car, the Cisitalia, to speed his return. Since then Porsche has consistently provided the company's design abilities to all manner of manufacturers.

Porsche's lasting fame, though, has come from the cars which the professor designed from start to finish – the rear-engined, air-cooled, road machines, and the largely mid-engined racing models. As demand increased in leaps and bounds for the Type 356, it became more luxurious to meet the needs of the largely American market, and the engines became bigger to give it an even more exciting performance. Porsches were always expensive cars but they offered exceptionally good value in that they were so well made and brought out the best – or the worst – in a driver.

Soon the Type 356 was winning its class in international racing because of that very handling, allied with exceptional streamlining that made it very fast for its size. It was only natural that Porsche should soon take to producing purpose-built racing cars. (These were called spyders, a name dating back to the time high-speed horse-drawn buggies scuttled along like spiders.)

Porsche had always been able to juggle its parts to produce highly competitive cross breeds of road and racing cars. It was tough, high-speed, machines like these that were so successful in rough road events such as the Carrera Panamericana in Mexico, and following these successes their highest-performance road machines were called Carreras. The gruelling Targa Florio mountain road race in Sicily also became a Porsche preserve when the tenacious spyders ran rings round far heavier, more powerful cars. When the Type 356 was refined into today's 911, it was only fitting that open versions should be called Targas.

Porsche has consistently succeeded in using racing as a development ground for road cars, the 911 starting from a Grand Prix-based engine, and continuing to its ultimate turbocharged form as a result of advances made in the building of the world's most awe-inspiring competition car, the 917. These machines, leading up to today's 956 and 962, have left all the others behind.

It was only natural that Porsche felt nervous about having so much of its future tied to the 911, a car whose original conception dates back to 1934. The company has experimented with mid-engine road cars, and will try again, but Porsche has also found a large market for more conventional machines: two front-engined GT cars, the bargain-priced 924 and the top-of-the-range 928. At one time it looked as though they might take over from the 911, but the demand seems never-ending for a traditional rear-engined Porsche. Porsche fans have never had it so good with such a choice – while the design department also manages to find time to produce the all-conquering TAG turbo engine in Formula 1!

1955 Porsche 550 Spyder

Porsche 356A coupé

During the early years of production, Porsche tended to make numerous detail changes almost at whim, as part of its constant search for perfection. But as the cars became more and more popular, this system became impractical. Engineers and designers could no longer halt the production line to make just one small change. Modifications had to wait until it was economical to do several at once. The result was that the Type 356 underwent no changes for six months until it was completely revised as the Type 356A in 1955! One of the main improvements was that the new cars were offered with an enlarged crankcase allowing an increase in engine capacity to 1600 cc. This provided not only more power for a better performance but also more torque, which made the car far easier to drive. It also took maximum advantage of the class capacity in Touring and Grand Touring car races.

The 1300 cc engines were retained for those who wanted to compete in the smaller classes, however. This meant that the Type 356A could be ordered with a 1300 cc unit producing just 44 bhp; a 1300S with 60 bhp; the new standard 1600 with 60 bhp; a 1600S on 75 bhp, and a new top model, the 1500GS Carrera, which had 100 bhp. This used a slightly detuned version of the Type 550's four-cam engine.

Many mechanical detail changes were made, some of them to create more refined running and others to give the units greater durability. The gearbox mountings, which had tended to break on very rough roads, were revised and so was the suspension, in keeping with the increased power. This work, including different anti-roll bar and torsion bar rates, needle-bearing pivots and better dampers, had been developed through the competition Porsches. The wheel rim width was also increased from 82.5 mm (3¼ in) to 114 mm (4½ in), which was considered quite daring at the time! Tyre firms were not at all sure that their products could put up with the punishment that would be meted out by a Porsche running on such wide rims – but with revisions to the steering, the Type 356A became much easier to drive than the earlier cars, as the former oversteer became a softer form of understeer. The car also looked quite different, now that Porsche could afford more expensive tooling: a new one-piece windscreen was introduced, and the floor was lowered to allow easier entry and exit.

ENGINE		CHASSIS	
Type	Flat, air-cooled	**Frame**	Platform chassis, integral with body
No. of cylinders	4		
Bore/stroke mm	82.5 × 74	**Wheelbase mm**	2100
Displacement cc	1582	**Track – front mm**	1306
Valve operation	Overhead, pushrod	**Track – rear mm**	1272
Sparkplugs per cyl.	1	**Suspension – front**	Independent, twin trailing arms, transverse torsion bars
Compression ratio	8.5:1		
Carburation	Two Solex carburettors		
BHP	75	**Suspension – rear**	Independent, swinging axles, twin trailing arms, torsion bars
Transmission	Four-speed manual gearbox		
		Brakes	Drums front and rear
		PERFORMANCE	
		Maximum speed	169 km/h (105 mph)
		Fuel consumption	9.42 litres/100 km (30 mpg)

1960 Porsche 356B cabriolet

Porsche 356B cabriolet

Production of the Type 356A continued for four years on the way to another complete revision into the 1959 Type 356B. The 1300 cc models were dropped in 1957 and a de luxe version of the Carrera offered with a heater and a slightly softer engine; this gave 10 bhp less, but made the car more docile to drive. The 1600S went over to quieter plain bearings, and the lower-output engine was given cheaper iron cylinders, which had much the same effect.

But the performance side was not neglected. The steering gear was modified again, and the 1600's twin exhausts were run through the rear over-riders to increase the ground clearance.

The accent was still towards improving comfort, however. A one-piece removable hardtop became available for the cabriolet and the Speedster, with better-quality interior fittings. The theory was also advanced that, although the Speedster was a cheap car by Porsche standards, it still cost a lot when compared to many others. Therefore, anyone who could afford to buy a Speedster could probably afford to buy a more luxurious car anyway. This argument appealed to Porsche in particular because of the higher profit margins involved. As a result, the Speedster was replaced by

the Speedster D (named after its bodybuilders, Drauz), which was well on the way to being a convertible, such was the quality of its trim. Following protests from California, though, to the effect that it wasn't a real Speedster, it was renamed the D-type Convertible!

Then, in 1958, the Carrera went up to 1600 cc and gained another 5 bhp before the Type 356B was introduced. This had a thoroughly Americanized nose with higher headlamps and much stronger bumpers mounted high both front and rear. As is often the case with a car developed specifically for the American market, the Type 356B weighed more. Its overall performance was little inferior, however, because its braking ability was improved. The interior was enlarged by surgery to the floorpan and a new engine was offered, the Super 90. This was a pushrod 1600 cc unit with nearly as much power as the Carrera's racing engine. In keeping with competition trends, the suspension on the top models was further improved by fitting Koni adjustable dampers and a camber compensating spring. A further attempt was made to quell the vocal minority in California by renaming the D-type Convertible the Roadster.

ENGINE		CHASSIS	
Type	Flat, air-cooled	Frame	Platform chassis, integral with body
No. of cylinders	4		
Bore/stroke mm	82.5 × 74	Wheelbase mm	2100
Displacement cc	1582	Track – front mm	1306
Valve operation	Overhead, pushrod	Track – rear mm	1272
Sparkplugs per cyl.	1	Suspension – front	Independent, twin trailing arms, transverse torsion bars
Compression ratio	8.5:1		
Carburation	Two Solex carburettors		
BHP	90	Suspension – rear	Independent, swinging axles, twin trailing arms, torsion bars
Transmission	Four-speed manual gearbox		
		Brakes	Drums front and rear

PERFORMANCE	
Maximum speed	185 km/h (115 mph)
Fuel consumption	10.46 litres/100 km (27 mpg)

1964 Porsche 356C Carrera 2 coupé

Porsche 356C Carrera 2 coupé

Extensive revisions were made to the Type 356B before it reached its ultimate form as the Type 356C. The Karmann coachbuilding company built a Roadster in the early 1960s and a hardtop version of it in 1961. Considerable changes were made to the construction of the bodies during this period, with an enlarged rear window for the coupé, a bigger engine cover and a larger luggage boot.

Soon the 75 bhp 1600S became known as the Super 75 and during 1962 it was fitted with the cheaper, sound-deadening cast iron cylinders used on the standard 1600. But the Carrera retained the all-alloy four-cam unit, which was enlarged to 2 litres in line with its relatives in the sports racing cars. Larger numbers were built to qualify this car, called the Carrera 2, for GT racing and rallying.

The revised body was carried over with minor modifications for the Type 356C in 1963. This had a number of refinements in the fittings, but most notably disc brakes front and rear, made by the Germany Ate company. They were basically of Dunlop origin, although one of their special features was the incorporation of a small drum in each rear disc to Porsche patents. This made the handbrake far more efficient than with normal disc applications.

New 15 in wheels were fitted with these brakes and further improvements were made to the suspension. The 1600, 1600S and Super 90 engines were replaced by the 1600C (on 75 bhp) and 1600SC (95 bhp) units. The 2000GS (or Carrera 2) remained unchanged.

The basic Type 356B floorpan had also been used from 1961 for another breed of GT racing machine, the Carrera GTL, which had a low-drag lightweight aluminium body. This was produced by the Italian-domiciled Austrian tuner, Carlo Abarth, who had collaborated with the Porsche family on the Cisitalia project. These cars with spyder-style trim weighed 140 kg (309 lb) less than a normal Carrera and were fitted with an engine tuned to produce 115 bhp in 1600 cc form and 130 bhp when the capacity went up to 2 litres. They were quite successful in special GT racing, just as the standard-bodied Carrera 2 excelled in rallies, winning its class in the 1963 Monte Carlo.

As a final permutation, a 2000GS-GT was produced in 1964 on the Type 356C Carrera 2 floorpan with a combination of the Abarth wedge-type nose and the spyder's rear bodywork!

ENGINE		CHASSIS	
Type	Flat, air-cooled	Frame	Platform chassis, integral with body
No. of cylinders	4		
Bore/stroke mm	90 × 74	Wheelbase mm	2100
Displacement cc	1966	Track – front mm	1306
Valve operation	Overhead camshafts	Track – rear mm	1272
Sparkplugs per cyl.	2	Suspension – front	Independent, twin trailing arms, torsion bars, anti-roll bar
Compression ratio	9.5:1		
Carburation	Two Solex carburettors	Suspension – rear	Independent, swinging axles, twin trailing arms, torsion bars, leaf spring
BHP	180		
Transmission	Four-speed manual gearbox		
		Brakes	Discs front and rear

PERFORMANCE	
Maximum speed	203 km/h (126 mph)
Fuel consumption	17.65 litres/100 km (16 mpg)

1971 Porsche 917 Kurz

Porsche 914/6

It seemed a very good idea when Volkswagen and Porsche decided to build a new sports car together. Porsche wanted a cheaper car to protect itself at that end of the market, while Volkswagen wanted to go upmarket with something sporty. Volkswagen had the capacity to make such a car and Porsche did not, although the Stuttgart company certainly knew how to design one. In addition, Volkswagen and Porsche had historic links and marketed each other's cars in many countries. So it needed only a handshake between Ferry Porsche and Heinz Nordhoff, Volkswagen's chief, to agree to build a 'Fourteener', the 914.

It would be mid-engined like contemporary competition machines because that seemed the best solution for a sports car. The cheap model would have Volkswagen running gear and a more expensive one would have more Porsche parts. In many areas the cheaper 914 would be known as a Volkswagen – except in the United States, where it was a Porsche for prestige reasons – with the more expensive car being a Porsche everywhere. One of the benefits to Porsche would be that Volkswagen could produce the bodyshell far more cheaply, and it was expected that it would cost

Porsche less as a result for its version, to be called the 914/6.

The layout went back to the very first Porsche with the engine ahead of the rear wheels and behind the seats. This made the car better balanced than a rear-engined design, but meant that there was less room for the driver and passengers. Only two seats were intended, however, so that did not seem to matter, and there was an advantage in luggage space.

The new car's shape was based on a design exercise by the German firm, Gugelot, that unfortunately lost many of its more attractive aspects in the interests of meeting numerous safety and environmental regulations. But it was nevertheless functional, with a Targa top and reasonable passenger compartment. The Porsche version used the running gear of the contemporary 911T, with coil springs at the back in place of torsion bars. Nordhoff, sadly, had died by the time it came out in 1969, and Volkswagen charged far more than anticipated for the bodyshell, making the car nearly the same price as the 911. As a result it did not sell well, largely because of its less attractive appearance. The Porsche 914 was axed in 1972, the Volkswagen version continuing until 1975.

ENGINE		CHASSIS	
Type	Flat, air-cooled	Frame	Platform chassis, integral with body
No. of cylinders	6		
Bore/stroke mm	80 × 66	Wheelbase mm	2450
Displacement cc	1991	Track – front mm	1361
Valve operation	Overhead camshafts	Track – rear mm	1382
Sparkplugs per cyl.	1	Suspension – front	Independent, wishbone and coil springs
Compression ratio	8.6:1		
Carburation	Two Weber carburettors	Suspension – rear	Independent, trailing arms, coil springs
BHP	110		
Transmission	Five-speed manual gearbox	Brakes	Discs front and rear
		PERFORMANCE	
		Maximum speed	206 km/h (128 mph)
		Fuel consumption	16.62 litres/100 km (17 mpg)

1972 Porsche 916

Porsche Carrera RS lightweight 2.7

The soaring costs of developing the 917 for sports car racing and the frequency with which regulations were changed to exclude cars of its type led to Porsche looking hard at other forms of competition for publicity, and as a stimulus to technical development. It was also apparent that cars such as the 917 were developing so fast that they bore little resemblance to road machines, which meant a loss in publicity. The answer was obvious: develop the road cars to a high pitch for international racing. This policy had not worked with the 914 in that sales had never risen to a profitable level, so Porsche's attention was turned once more to the 911. The existing 2.4-litre 911S was a formidable machine but rather too heavy to stay in front in GT racing, so the weight was reduced to 900 kg (1984 lb), mainly by drastic surgery on the trim. Mindful of the problems the company had experienced selling enough Speedsters, and the way in which any improvement in comfort was well received, Porsche thought it would have trouble selling the 500 cars it would have to build to qualify the new car for the appropriate class in international GT racing – so they decreed that every executive entitled to run a company car of such value would have to choose this model.

It was fitted with a bored-out 2.7-litre version of the 2.4-litre engine that was not in itself more powerful at 210 bhp, although it had more torque. However, the capacity could be further increased by intensive tuning to 2.8 litres for the optimum power output in competition. Various other modifications were made to the suspension and transmission aimed more at competition than anything else.

In a further attempt to give the RS 2.7, as the new model was named, a sales boost, Porsche resurrected the emotive old name Carrera. Imagine the surprise when the first production run of 500 was snapped up and the company had to run off another 536 to meet the demand!

RS Carreras were readily distinguished by their duck's tail spoilers to reduce rear end lift, front spoiler and dramatic side lettering. They came in three versions: the standard RS, a more highly-modified RSR just for racing, and the RST, with a more comprehensive trim package like the 911S, which was intended for touring. Almost by accident, Porsche had created what was to become one of its greatest classics, the fastest and lightest of the early 911s.

ENGINE		CHASSIS	
Type	Flat, air-cooled	Frame	Platform chassis, integral with body
No. of cylinders	6	Wheelbase mm	2271
Bore/stroke mm	90 × 70.4	Track – front mm	1372
Displacement cc	2687	Track – rear mm	1372
Valve operation	Overhead camshafts	Suspension – front	Independent, MacPherson struts, longitudinal torsion bars, anti-roll bar
Sparkplugs per cyl.	1		
Compression ratio	8.5:1		
Induction	Fuel injection	Suspension – rear	Independent, semi-trailing arms, transverse torsion bars, anti-roll bar
BHP	210		
Transmission	Five-speed manual gearbox	Brakes	Discs front and rear
		PERFORMANCE	
		Maximum speed	241 km/h (150 mph)
		Fuel consumption	18.83 litres/100 km (15 mpg)

1975 Porsche 930 (Turbo)

Porsche 935/78

The Type 935/78 raced in 1978 represented the 911 in its most advanced form. The first 935s were built to contest the sports car manufacturers' world championship (the World Championship of Makes) in 1976. This series was run under Group Five rules (hence the name 935), which stipulated that such machines must be based on a production car's bodyshell and cylinder block. The 930 was chosen as a base along with the near-standard 934 to race under Group Four regulations.

Under the Group Five formula, the bodyshell could be lightened and fitted with additional aerodynamic aids. This meant that Porsche was able to produce a car that looked quite like a 911 – which received good publicity as a result – but was far more stable at very high speeds. The 935's cause was helped when the governing body introduced a minimum weight limit in its class of 970 kg (2138 lb). Porsche had already reduced the weight to the same as the Carrera RS – 900 kg (1984 lb) – so the racing department was able to ballast the nose to provide an ideal racing weight distribution of 47 per cent front, 53 per cent rear. Other dramatic alterations included the use of ventilated disc brakes.

After overcoming problems with the specification of the turbo-charger intercoolers, the 935 easily won the Championship. Its main rival, BMW, was totally disheartened, especially when Porsche decided to continue in 1977 with higher-powered 935s to support the 936s in the World Sports Car Championship. More power was extracted from their 2.8-litre engines, and throttle lag reduced by the use of twin turbochargers, but the cars were plagued by cylinder head gasket failure all season. Nevertheless, the team won the manufacturers' championship again, but it gave Porsche little satisfaction, because the opposition had been so weak. They withdrew their works cars in 1978 and concentrated on Le Mans with the 936s and a 3.2-litre version of the 935 which had a permanent cure for that gasket problem: the new water-cooled four-valve cylinder heads were welded to the cylinder block! The bodyshell of this 935/78 had also been lowered by slicing off the bottom and rebuilding it around the driver's roll cage with a 936-style nose and tail. The appearance of this device on its test run at Silverstone was so dramatic that it was christened Moby Dick after the great white whale. It proved outstandingly fast, winning the British six-hour race, but failing to do so at Le Mans due to annoyingly minor problems.

ENGINE		CHASSIS	
Type	Flat, air-cooled cylinder blocks, water-cooled heads	Frame	Platform chassis, integral with body
No. of cylinders	6	Wheelbase mm	2271
Bore/stroke mm	95 × 74.4	Track – front mm	1502
Displacement cc	3160	Track – rear mm	1558
Valve operation	Overhead camshafts	Suspension – front	Independent, MacPherson struts, coil springs, anti-roll bar
Sparkplugs per cyl.	2		
Compression ratio	7:1		
Induction	Fuel injection, turbocharger	Suspension – rear	Independent, semi-trailing arms, coil springs, anti-roll bar
BHP	750		
Transmission	Four-speed manual gearbox	Brakes	Discs front and rear

PERFORMANCE	
Maximum speed	354 km/h (220 mph)
Fuel consumption	47.08 litres/100 km (6 mpg)

1980 Porsche 928S

Porsche 911 SC/RS rally car

Early Porsche 911s won the Monte Carlo Rally in lightweight 911T form, with 911S mechanical components. This was before the Carrera RS starred in the very tough East African Safari Rally as late as 1978 with its suspension raised to give 254 mm (10 in) ground clearance. After that, lightweight 911s began to perform well in rallycross, a combination of circuit racing and special stage rallying, benefiting from their great traction, with so much weight concentrated over the rear wheels. The cars' main problem was that they had so much power from engines up to 935 specification that the front wheels spent almost as much time in the air (as they hit huge bumps) as they did steering the cars.

The advent of four-wheel drive as a popular way of conveying a great deal of power to the ground became a priority as Porsche began to think again about how the 911 could be improved. As private teams in rallycross experimented successfully with their own four-wheel-drive systems, Porsche used cars built to compete in the 12070 km (7500 mile) Paris-to-Dakar desert rally for their development work. The winning combination, with Jacky Ickx at the wheel, was based on a standard 911 Carrera, its 3.2-litre engine running on a low compression ratio to cope with poor-quality fuel. Tall, high-profile, 205-section Dunlop desert racing tyres were fitted to normal alloy wheels with stilt-like suspension giving no less than 279 mm (11 in) of ground clearance. The standard MacPherson strut front suspension was replaced by less accident-prone wishbones using two dampers for each wheel; coil-sprung Turbo trailing links sufficed at the rear. Ventilated brakes were used all round and the chassis platform was reinforced to make an immensely rigid bodyshell that could withstand being bounced on its roof! To offset the extra weight, non-stressed body panels, such as the doors and wings, were made from glass-fibre. All manner of survival equipment was carried in a gutted interior behind the driver and navigator that could be reached through a metal lid which replaced the rear window.

The engine's 225 bhp was conveyed to the rear by normal means, with a 944 propeller shaft running forward to a 924 Turbo gearbox casing containing a freewheeling differential linked to the front wheels by drive shafts. This gave a power split of 30 per cent front, 70 per cent rear, which could be locked up for a 50/50 split on the 911 shown here winning the 1984 Paris-to-Dakar rally.

ENGINE		CHASSIS	
Type	Flat, air-cooled	Frame	Platform chassis, integral with body
No. of cylinders	6		
Bore/stroke mm	95 × 74	Wheelbase mm	2270
Displacement cc	3164	Track – front mm	1370
Valve operation	Overhead camshafts	Track – rear mm	1350
Sparkplugs per cyl.	1	Suspension – front	Independent, wishbone and coil springs
Compression ratio	7:1		
Induction	Fuel injection		
BHP	225	Suspension – rear	Independent, semi-trailing arms, torsion bars
Transmission	Five-speed manual gearbox		
		Brakes	Discs front and rear

PERFORMANCE	
Maximum speed	209 km/h (130 mph)
Fuel consumption	17.66 litres/100 km (16 mpg)

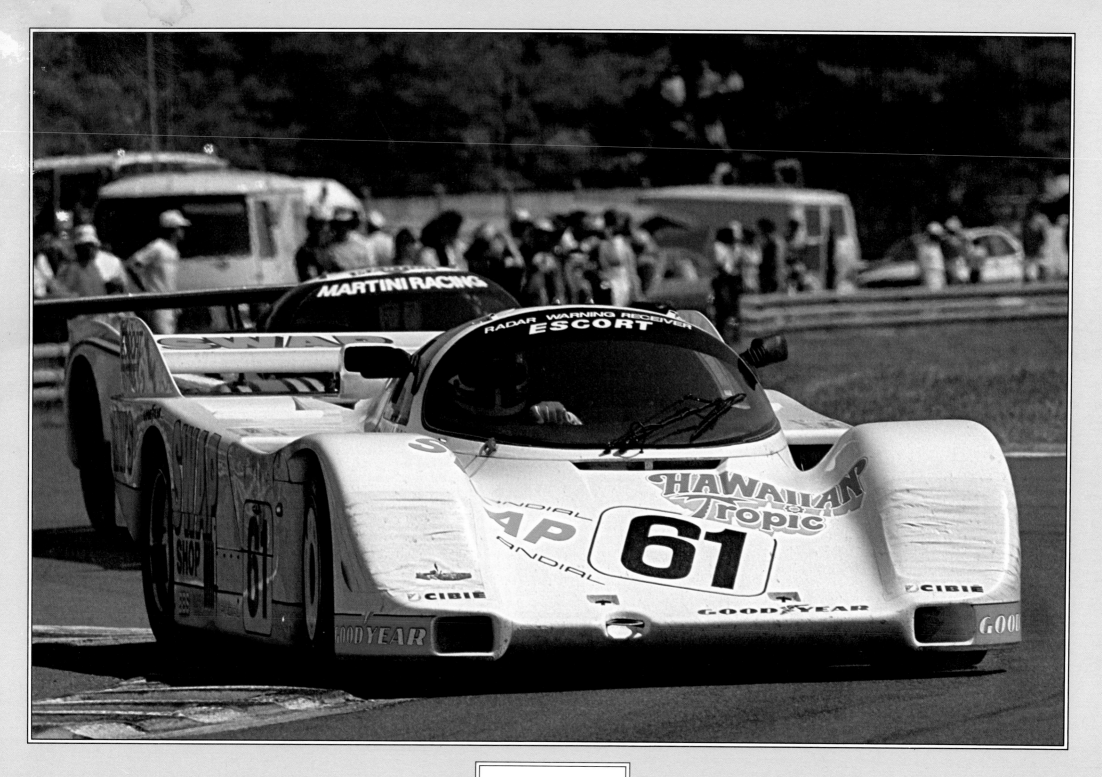

1984 Porsche 962

Porsche 962

Porsche's latest endurance racing car, the 962, is based closely on the all-conquering 956, and looks just the same. The main difference between Preston Henn's 962 – seen competing at Le Mans in 1984 – and the 956 is that the driver sits 102 mm (4 in) further back. This means that his feet are not in front of a line drawn between the hub centres. The change of position is dictated by American IMSA racing rules which decree that, although a 962 can race in Europe, a 956 cannot compete in American events!

The 956, and the 962, have become Porsche's most successful racing cars, dominating endurance events since the introduction of Group C rules in 1982 which rendered the 936 obsolete. In the new group there are no restrictions on the type of engine or capacity, the main factor being fuel consumption. This was initially confined to 50 litres/100 km (6 mpg). In addition, the regulations required a minimum weight of 800 kg (1737 lb) without fuel and a ban on aerodynamic aids such as wing-profiles, underbodies, and sealing skirts, that promote too high a cornering speed.

The 2.65-litre turbocharged four-valve engine used in the 936 was just able to meet the fuel consumption figures so it was developed for the 956 with a new type of fuel injection. In this form it still produced 620 bhp using a standard Porsche Turbo crankcase and shaft. But the torque was so great that a new five-speed gearbox had to be designed.

The 956 had the longest wheelbase seen on a Porsche racing car – 2649 mm (104¼ in) – because the new rules required overhanging bodywork not to exceed a set percentage of the wheelbase. It also had to be a closed car, unlike the 936, because of a minimum windscreen height of 1 m (39½ in).

The biggest departure for Porsche, however, was that it was the company's first full monocoque body, a method of construction pioneered on racing cars by Colin Chapman of Lotus 20 years earlier! Porsche had remained true to its spaceframes because they were light, efficient and easy to make. Monocoques are far more complex, but lend themselves better to providing a floor that generates maximum downforce and offers a higher degree of protection for the driver's feet in a crash.

Works 956s have won almost every race in which they have competed, scoring a hat trick of wins in the World Championship of Makes between 1982 and 1984. Their chief rivals come from the ranks of private teams running Porsche 956s and 962s!

ENGINE		CHASSIS	
Type	Flat, air-cooled cylinder block, water-cooled heads	Frame	Monocoque
		Wheelbase mm	2649
		Track – front mm	1580
No. of cylinders	6	Track – rear mm	1580
Bore/stroke mm	92.3 × 66	Suspension – front	Independent, wishbone and coil springs
Displacement cc	2650		
Valve operation	Overhead camshafts		
Sparkplugs per cyl.	1	Suspension – rear	Independent, wishbone and coil springs
Compression ratio	7.2:1		
Induction	Fuel injection, turbocharger		
		Brakes	Discs front and rear
BHP	600		
Transmission	Five-speed manual gearbox	**PERFORMANCE**	
		Maximum speed	362 km/h (225 mph)
		Fuel consumption	40.36 litres/100 km (7 mpg)